Research by Catherine McCarthy.

Designed by Stonecastle Graphics Ltd.

MALLARD PRESS

An imprint of BDD Promotional Book Company, Inc., 666 Fifth Avenue, New York, N.Y. 10103
Mallard Press and its accompanying logo are trademarks of BDD Promotional Book Company, Inc.

CLB2619
Copyright © 1990 Colour Library Books Ltd., Godalming, Surrey, England.
Copyright © 1990 Illustrations: Rex Features Ltd., and London Features International Ltd.
First published in the United States of America in 1990 by The Mallard Press.
Printed and bound in Italy.
All rights reserved.
ISBN 0 792 45423 6

NEW KIDS on the BLOCK

Edited by
Mike Clifford

ONCE UPON A TIME....

IF YOU like fairy tales, you're gonna love this one! Why, we've even got a fairy Godfather.

Picture "the man" Maurice Starr, disenchanted with his pet project New Edition, which he put together in 1983. Whilst they didn't take the charts by storm, the Massachusetts' based New Edition picked up a few hits including the UK #1 *Candy Girl* in 1983. Add to that a smattering of top forty hits in the US, and you have a group about to happen.

Then exit Maurice, resigned to a record deal he was not comfortable with, and then having to handle the loss of "your main man" Bobby Brown, the group's superstar vocalist. What Maurice did not need was another set of problems akin to New Edition. But then he didn't reckon on New Kids On The Block.

Maurice decided to soldier on and hunt down another New Edition. His determination was made keener by the solo success of Bobby Brown.

National advertising resulted in thousands of applicants to audition for this new band. The brief was short and to the point — "Talented young singers/dancers wanted. Must be good-looking".

Enter Donnie Wahlberg, whose upfront personality won over Maurice and his new partner Richard Scott, a former manager of Diana Ross.

Donnie was confident that his high school pals Danny Wood and brothers Jon and Jordan Knight could also cut it. Maurice agreed, and with the addition of teenybop Joe McIntyre, New Kids On The Block were finally born. Well, not quite.

The group (also from Massachusetts) was originally called Nynuk, and signed to CBS Records in early 1986. They were introduced to members of the press and television at a media launch for the July 4 Statue Of Liberty Celebrations that year.

Still known as Nynuk, the guys recorded their first album in 1988, after a couple of years on the road, where they appeared with a strange mix of acts like soul legends The Four Tops, as well as Lisa Lisa and Cult Jam.

The band's name change came in the studios, when, after laying down the vocals for a track called *New Kids On The Block,* both Maurice and Richard thought that this fitted the "street" image better. The Kids were born.

The first single from the *New Kids On The Block* was *Be My Girl,* a dance hit but only a taster of what was to come.

The title track from the lp was the quintet's next release, and this saw action in both the pop and soul charts in *Billboard* magazine.

All hell broke loose when *You Got It (The Right Stuff)* was released. Taken from the group's second album *Hangin' Tough* (1988), the Kids followed *Right Stuff* with two more mega hits, *I'll Be Loving You* (US #1) and the album title track *Hangin' Tough* (both UK and US#1).

In 1989 *Billboard* announced that NKOTB were the top artists for the year, with the *Hangin' Tough* set runner up to, ironically, Bobby Brown's *Don't Be Cruel* as album of the year.

A Christmas album *Merry Merry Xmas* secured massive airtime over the holiday period, and the group enjoyed a further hit with *This One's For The Children,* a radio favourite from the lp.

With the Kids so well established in the States, Maurice and Richard set a punishing tour schedule which would see the guys play in every State of the country, with audiences totalling over one million fans!

1990 saw NKOTB's first European gigs, where reaction was as crazy as the USA.

The sharp business brains of Maurice and Richard did not shut-off outside their music commitments, however.

New Kids On The Block is now a copyright logo which features on 12" life-like dolls (launched for Xmas, 1989), and a Hanna-Barbera cartoon series (upcoming Fall, 1990).

And don't forget the multi-million dollar deal with Coca-Cola, who sponsored the European tour. Coke's summer 1990 advertising campaign will feature New Kids On The Block, who follow other pop luminaries such as Madonna and Michael Jackson into the "soft drinks sell".

The future looks bright, despite the frantic changes associated with the pop business.

Movies are a cert, and we predict a flurry of solo projects. Whatever happens, New Kids On The Block have repaid the resolution of Maurice Starr and have turned Boston, Mass. into one of the hippest cities in the USA.

Donnie

DONNIE (real name Donald) Wahlberg was born in Boston, Massachusetts on the 17th August, 1969, one of the youngest of a large family — and he has three sisters (Debbie, Tracey and Michelle), and four brothers (Paul, James, Arthur and Robert)!

His hectic upbringing has led Donnie to appear serious and reserved, and he often hides behind round wire-framed glass offstage — shades of John Lennon.

But when he's funkin' it out with the band — watch out! This Kid's a flirt and a mover when the band starts biting.

Donnie is not backward in coming forward when NKOTB are in full flow. Nearly six feet tall, with mousey blond hair and hazel eyes, his looks are a formula for female flirtatiousness. And if you think that this Kid they call "Cheese" is not aware of the fluttering hearts he causes, you ain't for real!

Donnie is one of the original members of NKOTB — he met Jon, Jordan and Danny way back in '75 at primary school in Boston, and even then they stuck together as a group, for better, but usually, for worse! Donnie and school didn't really mix, but at least he knew it was better than bumming on the street.

What else do we know about young Mr. Wahlberg?

Well, you'll never find him out of his favourite sneakers, and he's happiest dressed in a Levi jacket and dark sweatshirt. He's a keen sports fan, and loves the Boston Celtics basketball team and the Boston Red Sox baseball squad.

Music? Donnie likes the soul beat, and would probably say "Janet Jackson" if you asked him to name his favourite singer.

Donnie is also keen on movies, although he has to stay home — he recently bought a large house — and watch them on video now.

He's a big Al Pacino fan, and cites "Scarface" as his top flick. And if he was offered a part in a film, he would like Cher to co-star. Get in the queue!

Joe

THIS KID'S still a teenager, and was born Joseph Mulrey McIntyre on the last day of December 1972, in Needham, Massachusetts. His nickname is "Bird", 'cos he's always "birddoggin'"!

Joe is a real kid — five feet six and growing, with a wiry frame he throws around stage with great abandon! He's treated like a little brother by the rest of the Kids.

If light brown hair and blue eyes are your ideal combo, Joe is your man. The second youngest of a large Irish family — six, yes, six sisters (Jean, Carol, Kaye, Tricia, Alice and Judy) and one brother (Thomas) — Joe had to hang tough for a piece of the family action. That's what made him the independent man he is.

If you sense a guarded nature, put that down to dad, a gritty union negotiator who was always looking for the best for his men. Joe's the same way. Mess with the Kids, and he'll mess with you!

When the serious business stops, mind out where you sit or stand. Joe has probably left some gum around, or squirted foam in your favourite sneakers!

Like the rest of NKOTB, Joe is crazy about sports, but he prefers the bowling alley to the basketball court.

Surprisingly, Joe is a heavy metal fan. Well, he is the youngest! Watch out for the thunderous sound of Twisted Sister if you visit his house! And when the record player's off, a De Niro movie is on! And his favourite actress is sister Judith.

Joe is a jeans and t-shirt guy, with a trunk full of Nike trainers. Don't you DARE part him from those sneakers!

Donnie reckons he and Joe argue a lot — they both have to be right. But Joe did give Donnie some valuable advice when it comes to the ladies. "Splash on the Paco Raban, man, it drives 'em crazy", he reckons.

Jon

JONATHAN Rashleigh Knight is Jordan's older brother. He's the veteran of the group, and was born in Worcester, Massachusetts on the 29th November, 1968.

A rangy five feet eleven inches tall, with dark brown hair and hazel eyes, Jon has acquired two strange nicknames — Jizz or "The Rinse".

He won't say where they came from. Sensible man! Rashleigh, by the way, was his grandmother's family name. Look up Jordan for the family background.

Feed Jon Italian food, and he'll follow you anywhere. Most likely you'll find him on the end of a strand of spaghetti after a NKOTB concert.

And, whilst he's eating, Jon likes tranquility. Turn up the volume, and you'll get a look as black as, well, night!

Jon is reckoned to be the shyest member of the band, and suffered from stage fright when NKOTB first played live gigs.

But now he's comfortable in his surroundings. Long-time friends Donnie and Danny, plus brother Jordan, moved

as a pack in school. They've been tight ever since, and Jon is content in this "family" relationship.

Jon's controlled vocals feature on the Kids' love songs, and don't think that happened by accident. "The fans think he's kinda shy" says Donnie. "He's perfect for the smoochie stuff."

Another sports buff, Jon likes to swim in Summer and ski in Winter. Where does he find the time? Well, he doesn't anymore — a holiday please, Maurice! Someday he'll need to buy his own mountain to enjoy the piste in peace and quiet!

Music is another matter. Turn it up, bro'! As long as it's not heavy metal, that is. The racoons of rock are a real no-no as far as this Kid is concerned.

Like brother Jordan, Jon is a Robert De Niro fan. And, still with the movies, try tearing him away from his James Dean sweatshirts!

Jon's other hobby is walking his pet Boston Terrier "Wrinkles", and this tough little pooch helps keep cats away — Jon is allergic to their fur!

Like the rest of NKOTB, Jon thinks he'll eventually quit show business and live in the lap of luxury in Hawaii. Save us a place, you guys!

ERIC EASTON
THE SENSATIONAL
ROL
STO
THE CHECK
SPENCER DA
UNIT FOU

Jordan

JORDAN Nathaniel Marcel Knight – you can call him Jordan – is tall, dark and, yes preeeettttttyyyy handsome. Five feet ten, with dark brown hair and eyes, this Kid is a native of Worcester, Massachusetts, and first saw the light of day on the 17th May, 1970.

Apart from brother Jon – another Kid – Jordan has two sisters (Sharon and Allison) and two other brothers (David and Chris).

NKOTB think Jordan's a "smoothie", and he certainly handles himself well when the going gets tough. Put that down to a solid family upbringing. Jordan's dad is a priest, and he

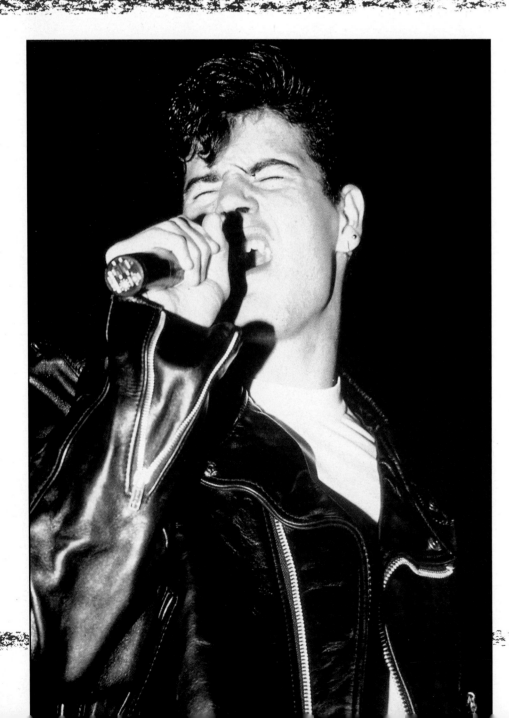

hammered home what side of the line to stand on! Sadly, the family was split apart when their mother and father decided to separate.

Don't think, however, that Jordan was an angel at school. He got into his fair share of trouble, and paid plenty of visits to the Principal's office.

He learnt his music at summer camp at the Royal School Of Church Music at Princeton University, and stuck it out even when the teachers teased him about his breakdancing prowess in class breaks!

The Kid they call "Jay" is another sports fan. He swims and plays basketball, but he's given up walking so he can cruise in his new Porsche 911 – mmm, mmm!

At home, Jordan likes to turn up the music loud, and he'll usually reach for a Prince or One Nation album. He says he also likes Maurice Starr's cuts – no wonder he's in the band!

Like the rest of the guys, he's also a movie buff, and will happily settle for anything starring Robert De Niro.

Jordan's wardrobe is full of loafers, trainers, leather jackets and denims. Whatever's hot on the street will meet with Jay's approval.

He reckons his one bad habit – biting nails – could be cured by a year long vacation on his favourite island Hawaii. Trouble is, he'd find a million girls trying to help him mend his ways!

Danny

THE MAN they call "puff" was born Daniel Wood, on the 14th May, 1969 in Boston Massachusetts, part of another large New England family — he has four sisters (Rachel, Melissa, Pamela and Bethany) and a brother (Brett). Danny's father, incidentally, works for the US Postal Service.

A solid five feet seven and a tiny bit, Danny is crazy about weights, and will lift just about anything he can get his hands on.

Personal trainer Butch makes Danny train at every opportunity, even on the road. Butch reckons this kid could have his job as a bodyguard at ANY time!!

Those powerful shoulders and arms, coupled with jet black hair and deep brown eyes make the tough Kid a throwback from "West Side Story".

Danny was a real street urchin, and got into plenty of trouble as a teenager.

School was no better, and he and the other Kids at the time — Donnie, Jon and Jordan — paid frequent visits to that office upstairs!

But Danny was no clown, and excelled at maths, and was later offered a place at Boston University. He was also a great sportsman, and captained the school football team.

Because Danny learned the hard way, he now has no time for street crime — "If we can break out of the mould, so can anyone" he says. In fact, the only thing he now likes about the city blocks is the fashion. It's got to be a leather or denim jacket, tight fitting cords and the latest sneakers.

And talking of tight fitting pants, wouldn't you just know that Danny has a habit of splitting them onstage!

When he's not working out or pumping iron, Danny likes to listen to David Bowie, or watch any movie with Kevin Costner or Cher.

He's another Kid with misty eyes for Hawaii. Hey guys, ever thought of buying the place?

ON THE STREET

"WHEN THE singing's got to stop, the pop star has to shop". For clothes, that is. And, although you can't see them when you buy that latest album or CD, the rock idol's wardrobe is nearly as important as the music.

"Street" fashions are nothing new, but New Kids On The Block have turned them into an art form. Whatever's right on the block is right for the show.

Pop fashion has seen extraordinary trends since the mid-fifties, starting with those rock 'n rollers in their Italian Suits, through flower power in the sixties to punk and precious in the seventies, and then 'anything goes' in the eighties.

NKOBT are leading the nineties with 'natural' (like mom's apple pie and ice cream). No put up job here. Guide, producer and mentor Maurice Starr was told firmly that their image would be for real. "We wear what the kids can wear", they said. And did.

T-shirts and denim, sneakers or loafers. The odd earring. Ponytails (Jordan and Danny, with Donnie making a REAL effort). Razor cut hairstyles. Leather jackets. Like any guys on the corner of the block.

The secret of the pop star's closet is style, whether it's Gucci punk — Blondie or Madonna, or manicured modern — Duran Duran, Culture Club. Even the heavy metal bands make some effort. However, they dress BEFORE being hit by a truck. Or so it seems.

The Kids have made no apology for their look. You might occasionally catch Jon in a dark suit, but it's usually a leather jacket from his vast collection. Danny favours sweatshirts and jeans. Joe won't be parted from his Hornets basketball jacket. Donnie is a t-shirt and denim man. Jordan switches from Levi jacket and sweatpants to studded bikers jacket and denims, or a Boston Celtics satin bomber jacket PLUS woolly socks!

All the guys wear sneakers, probably Nikes but occasionally Adidas. If they need to be business smart, watch out for the two-tone brogues or crepe soled suedes. If they're comfortable, pack 'em in the suitcase.

With the exception of street styles, clothes are usually 'in' or 'out'. And that's a big expense, and one which NKOTB are not comfortable with. When you dress to a budget, the t-shirt is your best friend.

The Kids know that albums/CD's/concert tickets/teen magazines take their toll of the allowance. Why burden their fans more?

The street has survived since Marlon Brando in 'On The Waterfront' and, a little later, 'West Side Story'. The Kids intend to maintain the tradition. You have their word for it.

NKOTB

ALTHOUGH New Kids On The Block have "grown up" since the release of their self-titled first album in 1986, there is plenty to admire in this 10 track collection.

Maurice Starr's well-balanced production has some outta sight moments. Let's look at the music:

Side one opens with the uptempo *Stop It Girl,* which features a hunky synthesized voice. Track two is a cute cover version of the Delfonics *Didn't I (Blow Your Mind).* This is followed by two teen anthems, *Popsicle* and *Angel.* You just KNOW what they're about! The final cut on the top side is the sixties soul-styled *Be My Girl.* What a question!!

The song that made it ALL happen, *New Kids On The Block,* introduces side two. This funky rap is resplendent with dub D.J. effects. Real cookin'! The guys lay some street talk on us in *Are You Down,* before we hear some smooth soul sounds on *I Wanna Be Loved By You.* Song number four is *Don't Give Up On Me,* featuring the misty vocals of Phaedra Butler. The album closes with the easy rocking *Treat Me Right,* with the guys harmonising over a seventies skipbeat.

Amazingly, *New Kids On The Block* has never been released outside of the States, although demand has meant that both the CD and cassette have found their way into Europe and Japan.

For the fact freaks amongst you, the album was written and arranged by Maurice Starr, with the exception of *Didn't I (Blow Your Mind)* and *Are You Down.*

The smokin' sounds were recorded at Mission Control, House of Hits and Newbury Sound (all Boston, Mass.), Eastern Sound (Methuen, Mass.) and Normandy Sound (Warren, Rhode Island).

NKOTB's debut lp "New Kids On The Block".

HANGIN' TOUGH

NEW KIDS ON THE BLOCK

HANGIN' TOUGH

EPD 6036

"Hangin' Tough" was NKOTB's second album.

HANGIN' TOUGH was NKOTB's second album, but the first released on both sides of the Atlantic. Suffice to say, the guys think it's a thousand times better than *New Kids On The Block*, their debut lp.

... HANGIN' TOUGH

All tracks were arranged and produced by the group's mentor and manager Maurice Starr. Maurice also played all the instruments as well as programming the synthesizers. He may have even cooked the lunches if time wasn't pressing.

Here's a track-by-track rundown. Do you think we're biased?

Side One

1. *The Right Stuff.* Yes, the single that made it ALL happen. A sparse, funky backing track is held together by a thunderous synthesized bass. NKOTB can really lay their vocal sound on us, as nothing, but nooooothing is allowed to hinder the pertinent message, "You've got the right stuff baby...". Maurice's ear for a clever instrumental sound is well illustrated by the sharp choral-like keyboard — you remember church now, don't you?

2. *Please Don't Go Girl.* A lovely Jackson 5-style ballad. Yes, I know NKOTB are not keen on comparisons, but this is flattering. Joe's great lead vocal is boosted by some superb harmonies on the phrase "...always will". Listen out for them. And Joe's soulful singing is right there with the regimental high-hat drum sound.

3. *I'll Be Loving You (Forever).* For the music students amongst you, this soul ballad is played to strict 4/4 time (1,2,3,4 and 1,2,3,4 — get it?) with tympani-type drum fills. Those who are old enough to remember Little Anthony and the Imperials may make a favourable comparison. I certainly did! A perfect choice for the Spring single. And, hey, how did Jordan make that high note at the end of the song? Wow!!!

4. *Cover Girl.* This is a hard drivin' rock 'n roll track with a hair-raising guitar solo. Maurice has also given the song a chug-a-lug beat featuring a fairground organ sound. He must be as old as me, because this reminded me of Chris Montez' great sixties pop hit "Let's Dance". A fantastic dance number, kept going by a frantic bass passage near the end. The Kids work the vocals well, reminding us about their dream magazine "cover girl".

5. *I Need You.* An uptempo ballad featuring a lovely melodic guitar solo by Maurice, with the Kids' sharp vocals highlighted by a spoken passage at the end of the track. And so ends side one. Please turn the music over!

The inner sleeve from "Hangin' Tough" album.

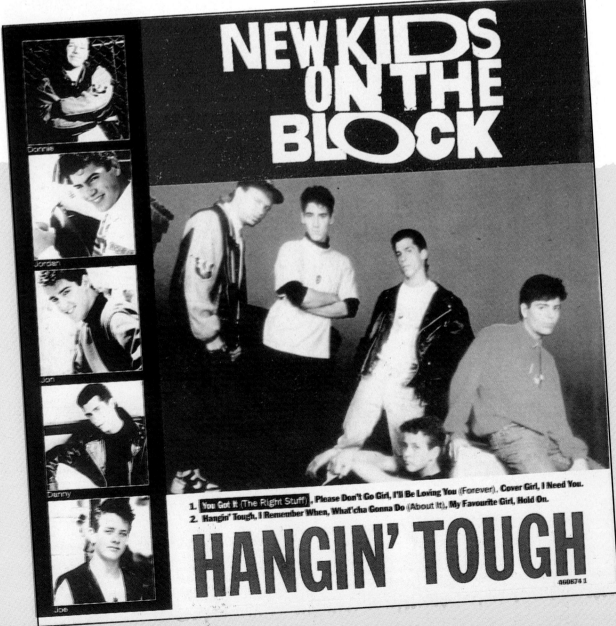

Side Two

1. *Hangin' Tough.* Oh, oh, here we go! Tough synthesized bass, loads of whistles and a steady hi-hat sound take the Kids through your favourite track. You bought zillions when it was released as a single. I like the bass pattern which follows the melody, and the sixties Jimmy Smith-style organ solo. Then we get the modern keyboard sound, before the fade out with what sounds like a motorbike revving.

2. *I Remember When.* It's gotta be said, but this sounds uncannily like an early Jackson 5 track. A poignant ballad which Joe does not spare the horses on. Where does he get that energy? Maurice adds a nice clavinet sounding synthesizer on the fade out.

3. *What'cha Gonna Do About It.* I'll tell ya what I'm gonna do. I'm gonna GET DOWN. This is funk, funk, funk, and I'm dancing as I'm writing. Love that staccato synthesized bass, and then the guitar and keyboards during the chorus. Jordan speaks to us at the end — "I know you still love me", quiver, quiver!!!

4. *My Favourite Girl.* A heavy pop number which is strung out over a vibrant bass pattern. Great chorus and a neat mini synthesized drum solo with outta space style keyboards. Been watching those Star Wars movies again, Maurice???

5. *Hold On.* This starts with a rhythmic bass, and a solid bass drum backing. And then Maurice lets rip with a heavy metal guitar solo, with lots, and I mean lots, of echoooooooo!! Did I hear shades of Earth Wind and Fire in the synthesized brass solo? Hey, hang on, here comes that guitar again! You auditioning for Guns And Roses Maurice?

New Kids On The Block with manager Dick Scott.

TOUGH FACTS...

All the songs on "Hangin' Tough" were written by Maurice Starr, except "I Remember When" (Maurice, Eban Kelly and Jimmy Randolph) and "My Favourite Girl" (Maurice, Donny, Jordan and Danny).

Maurice Starr Music publishes the material, except "I Remember When", which is published by Maurice Starr Music and Urban Groovy Tunes.

Danny, Jordan and Donny were official Associate Producers. Way to go, guys!

Danny also got his hands on the DMX programming for "My Favourite Girl".

The album was recorded at Mission Control, in Westford, Massachusetts, The House Of Hits, in Boston, Massachusetts and Normandy Recording Studio, Providence, Rhode Island.

CHILLIN' OUT

BEDLAM! New Kids On The Block are onstage, and ALL hell has broken loose.

Fans are trying to break through the barrier of muscular human flesh that's protecting our heroes from the wilder element in the crowd. These Rambo lookalikes don't frighten anyone. Nor do they want to. Just a peaceful evening please. No chance. These fans are WIIIIIILD!!

Before the show starts, NKOTB host an informal "beer/coke/sandwiches" gathering with local press and TV personalities. Some of the CBS Record executives are present, keeping a close watch on their most valuable asset. And for a few loyal fans, this is a dream come true. Competition winners, and those just lucky enough to be in the right place at the right time, have an opportunity to brush shoulders with our famous five.

The Kids are relaxed. Jon is wrestling with Danny, who's just boxed with Donnie, who's hair was tugged by Joe. You get the picture. These are young guys, aware of the attention bestowed upon them, but still young enough to enjoy a good time. These are REAL kids. Your mom's gonna LOVE 'em. Well, maybe not the ponytails.

With less than an hour to go before showtime, NKOTB start getting serious. "Let's chill 'em out tonight", says Danny. He knows they will anyway, but he wants this concert to be special. The band know that fans have been let down many times by the latest 'teenybop' sensation who don't, or can't, deliver on stage. Let me tell you, if the rap is that the Kids are just a hyped bunch of no-talents, they are wrong, wrong, wrong. They are cool dancers, polished singers. The material is great. And they're getting better.

The stage clothes are being laid on hangers. The stuff looks like their regular street gear, but with a sharper crease. In an hour, it will be soaked with sweat, or maybe ripped into shreds by the adoring masses. Donnie once threw an expensive sequined jacket into the crowd. They did get it back later. All 16 pieces!!

For tonight's show, Joe is wearing a red sweatshirt over a white t-shirt, with faded denims. Danny has found a hat — shades of Frank Sinatra — whilst Jordan has a shiny silver waistcoat under a black jacket. He was wearing a coloured bandana, but that's just a memory; a special souvenir for some lucky lady. Donnie looks real street. Denim from head to toe, with multi-coloured sweatshirt and copper pendant. Jon is supercool, just like you read in the fan magazines. Blue shirt and jeans, and with a broad smile that never fades.

Our super 'live' shots of NKOTB show just how varied their stage outfits can be. Monday, t-shirts and jeans...Tuesday, suits with waistcoats...Wednesday, sweatshirts and sneakers...

The Kids are working hard, bro. Struttin', jumpin'. Non-stop action. There is a deafening roar then the opening bars of 'You Got It (The Right Stuff)' are heard. And then absolute craziness when 'Hangin' Tough' is pounded out. Some of the audience are overwhelmed, most tearful, all with their special favourites. Jon is the King tonight, but tomorrow...?

Danny Wood, who says he still gets butterflies before he goes on stage, is pleased, "Good show guys. Way to go".

Some of the gifts that the fans have thrown onstage are laid out on a table, vying for space with empty Pepsi cans and half-eaten burgers. Many unmentionables, but some rock 'n roll teddys, scarves, letters. The list is endless.

"Maybe they'll throw some Nintendo Games", says Joe. Nintendo is the TV arcade machine that the Kids get off on. And believe you me, they need to wind down. Lucky that the homework has already been done!

The next morning, the bus is ready to take NKOTB to the next show. Danny has been working out in the hotel gym. He's superfit. Joe has struggled with his breakfast. He's supertired.

Another day, another gig. Next week they're in your town. You hope!

Jordan

Danny

Joe

Donnie

BUS OR PLANE? A simple choice, determined by NKOTB's parents, who decided that their boys would be safer on the ground when travelling from concert to concert. If you think it's a tough life, their specially equipped coach has a bar, video and TV and Nintendo games machine. Whilst it doesn't make the journeys shorter, it eases the pain.

THE KIDS HAVE become compulsive shoppers, and love checking out toy stores for the latest gimmicks and gizmos. Donnie reckons they'll need a warehouse to store all the games they bought during their recent American tour.

YOU'RE NO FAN of the Kids if you take drugs. So say the whole group, who were prime participants in Nancy Reagan's "Just Say No" anti-drugs campaign. NKOTB take their involvement seriously, because all the guys have had friends who have suffered because of substance abuse.

Their fervent campaigning earned them a special honour when Michael Dukakis, Governor of Massachusetts, named April 24 1988 "New Kids On The Block Day".

STAY OUTTA TOWN if the Kids are on a promo tour. New York was practically closed when the boys hit the City to sign a contract for the new Hanna-Barbera cartoon series upcoming this Fall. 20,000 fans surrounded the Hard Rock Cafe where the signing session took place. NKOTB escaped via a restaurant roof and down an adjacent fire escape!

NEW KIDS ON THE BLOCK have already made their presence felt in the charity field, helping hospitals in and around Boston with gifts of stuffed animals, and they made a timely appearance on a telethon in the States for the United Cerebral Palsy charity.

THE RUMOURS STILL abound. We heard that the Kids are black! And that they were killed in a plane crash (we KNOW they go by bus). Then split up before their UK tour. Drugs and more

drugs. Well, they're not perfect, but deserve better than this. Believe it when you hear it from the guys' own lips!

WHILST THE KIDS say they won't date their fans, don't despair. "You can never say never", says Danny, giving hope to millions of young ladies!

And talking of dating, Jon and Tiffany are still a hot item. Hankies to the ready girls!

GOTTA PEN? Wanna help out with the fan mail? NKOTB receive over 25,000 letters a day. You'll need a lot of lead in that pencil.

THE US AND UK fan clubs have nearly 200,000 members, and that's probably just the tip of the iceberg.

NEW KIDS ON THE BLOCK'S telephone chat line in the States costs two dollars a minute, and the 'phone company reckons nearly three million people have dialled. Or is that one person three million times!

THE GUYS HARDLY HAVE time for pets anymore, although Jon can be seen around town with his Boston Terrier. Quiz — why a BOSTON Terrier?

SO WHERE DOES ALL the money go? Well, the Kids prefer to buy for other people. Joe bought his mom a fur coat, Donnie bought a house, whilst Danny and both Jordan and Jon helped renovate their parents' homes. Nice touch, fellas!

JOE HAS TO TAKE classes every day, because he can no longer go to high school. "It's tough when I see the other guys havin' fun", he says. But he just knows it's gotta be done.

FIVE'S THE RIGHT NUMBER for a basketball team, so NKOTB try to find a court when they have a spare moment. Can ya dunk, fellas!

WHEN NEW KIDS ON THE BLOCK are on the West Coast or in Florida, they head for Disneyworld. They are CRAZY about cartoons. And now they're stars of their own 'toon!

KIDOLOGY

WE ARE THE MAIN MEN !!

NEW KIDS ON THE BLOCK are not usually troubled, or even annoyed, by the media. But there is one question, asked at EVERY press conference, which drives the guys crazy (mad, that is). And it is:

"What do you think when people compare you to the Osmonds?" Yell, scream, abuse, then hasty exit. By the reporter!

Okay, we may be unfair, but let's look at the background of the Osmonds and another group — the Jackson 5 — which our heroic five might find revealing. And then they can throw us out.

The Osmonds were formed way back in 1960, by, at that early stage, four brothers, Alan, Wayne, Merrill and Jay Osmond.

Talented musicians — a fact often overlooked by their critics — the group started out as a dance band at Disneyland in Los Angeles, where they were spotted and signed for a residency on Jerry "Great Balls Of Fire" Lee Lewis' tv show.

When Donny, then aged nine, joined the group, they were on the fringe of a recording career which resulted in a dozen hit singles.

Donny also enjoyed success as a solo artist, as did younger sister Marie, and baby brother Jimmy.

At the end of the seventies, the group were struggling to sustain the frantic adulation which had seen them take the pop world by storm. It is no exaggeration to say that they were THE most popular group from that era, in terms of media and fan attention.

Incredibly, the Jackson 5's career was almost a mirror image of the Osmonds. The five brothers, led by Michael, turned the pop world on its head in 1970, when *I Want You Back* soared to No 1 in the US charts, and No 2 in the UK listings.

Throughout the decade, the family — later known as The Jacksons — scored hit after hit after hit.

Although he has always officially been a member of the Jacksons, Michael's solo career has been another epic of fan euphoria and multi-million selling albums.

And, despite a much-ridiculed lifestyle, he has maintained his reputation as a megastar, with each rare record release eagerly awaited. Sister LaToya has, of course, also emulated much of her brothers' glory.

What New Kids On The block do NOT share with either the Osmonds or Jacksons is that they are not a complete family unit, although Jon and Jordan are brothers.

Ironically, the family backgrounds of both of those superstar groups was unable to prevent splits within the ranks.

Ultimately, NKOTB will need to sustain their drive and ability on several fronts. Neither The Jacksons (as a group) nor Osmonds were successful in movies, although Donny and Marie Osmond had faltering film careers. Michael Jackson is almost certain to establish himself in cinema, having already given hints of his talent on celluloid in the *Thriller* video and as *Captain E-O* in the 3-D movie exclusively screened at the Disney theme parks in Florida and California. NKOTB look tailor made for the big screen, and plans are already afoot for a movie in 1991.

The Kids certainly have the looks and talent to survive. But it is a jungle out there, and luck plays an important part. And, hey, they may not want to be around as a group in the years to come! Chances are that continued success will demand it.

Unlike the Osmonds or Jacksons, only Jordan (left) and Jon (right) are REAL brothers.

AND IN MY CRYSTAL BALL...

A QUESTION and Answer session about the probable future of New Kids On The Block.

WHEN WILL THE NEXT ALBUM BE RELEASED?

NKOTB had a hectic touring schedule during the winter of 1989/90, but should be off the road by April, 1990. Then it's back into the studio to tidy up existing tracks and lay down new cuts. We reckon early Fall this year will see a new Kids album. So do CBS Records, and they should know!

HOW LONG WILL THE "STREET" LOOK LAST?

Years, and years, and years. T-shirts and jeans are nothing new. James Dean was wearing them in the fifties. What the Kids are doing is refining the look. It's still "street". It's still in. And ten years down the road, nothing will have changed.

ARE THE KIDS GONNA BE MOVIE STARS?

Yes, probably a year and a bit from now. Contrary to rumours, the Hanna-Barbera cartoon series is PURE animation. Our guys will not feature (except their voices). But the movie scripts are pouring through Maurice Starr's letterbox, and he's going to make a decision soon.

We think that the guys will feature in a non-musical role, and it may be REAL serious. Forget the beach movie stuff. And waaaay down the road, Jon has those sultry looks that the camera just adores. Tom Cruise, eat your heart out!

WILL NKOTB EVER GO SOLO?

Of course they will! The secret is when?

Look at it this way. The Jacksons stuck it out for 15+ years, and the Osmonds for a decade. This is early days for NKOTB, although they do have solo projects they would like to start off.

Look to Jon as a producer. And maybe Joe with an Xmas single. Donnie could cut it on a tv series. Danny and Jordan will dance the night away — in a stage special?

HOW ABOUT A TV SPECIAL?

Yes, and definitely. Too good an opportunity to miss. How about this winter? And, no, Perry Como will NOT be a guest!

ARE THE KIDS GETTING MARRIED?

Maybe. Someday. Jon likes Tiffany. The rest of the guys are maintaining a discreet silence. We say let 'em enjoy their youth. Do a lotta living. And THEN settle down. But don't panic, no-one's engaged — yet!

WHERE WILL THE NEXT VIDEO BE SHOT?

After the cars in "You Got It (The Right Stuff)" and warehouse in "Hangin' Tough", what's next on the video agenda? Depends on the song. But we know you fans love seeing them live. How about shots from their recent American tour?

WILL JORDAN, DANNY AND DONNIE CUT OFF THEIR PONYTAILS?

Sure. We got the rights to sell those locks of hair! Fashion is fickle, and they may get them torn off before long.

WHAT DO THE KIDS THINK THEY'LL BE DOING IN 20 YEARS TIME?

Danny thinks he'll be "real old, but not forgotten!" Jon intends to keep in step with whatever's happening on the street. He'll do that till he's seventy! "I dunno what's happening *next* year. Let's wait and see', says Jordan. Joe wants to finish school, and experience life. Donnie figures he'll go out in a blaze of glory, just like Jimmy Dean...Just kiddin', folks!

WHAT ARE THE KIDS' OWN HOPES FOR THE FUTURE?

The end of the threat of nuclear war...That Maurice Starr reforms his own band Zapp...The fans in Europe go as ape as those in the USA...That people remember it's THEIR voices on the cartoon show...And peace and happiness to one and all.

Donnie

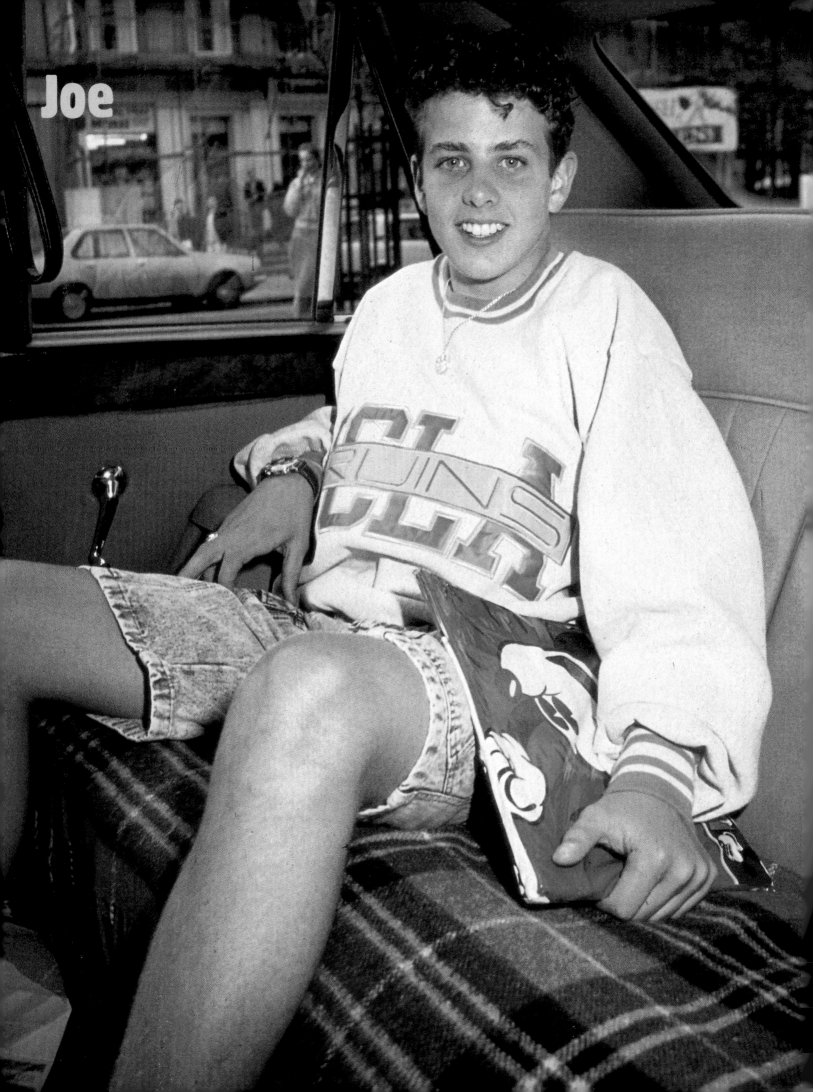

Joe

Jordan

Danny

STAYING IN TOUCH

LISTED below are NKOTB fan club addresses for both the USA and UK. Don't forget to enclose an International Reply Coupon if you're writing from outside the States

USA:

New Kids On The Block
PO Box 7001
Quincy
Massachusetts 02269
USA

UK:

New Kids On The Block
52 Gover Court
Paradise Road
London SW4 6QT
England

NKOTB albums/singles/CDs/tapes are released by CBS Records. They can be contacted at the following addresses:

USA:

CBS Records Inc
51 W 52nd Street
New York NY10019
USA
Telephone (212) 445 4321

UK:

CBS Records
17 Soho Square
London W1
England
Telephone: (071) 734 8181

The group's US management company is:

Dick Scott Entertainment Inc
159 West 53rd Street
Suite 11A
New York NY10019
USA

12" life-like NKOTB dolls!